MEDUSA

DEBORAH NOURSE LATTIMORE

JOANNA COTLER BOOKS

An Imprint of HarperCollins*Publishers*

AUTHOR'S NOTE

From the earliest times mankind has told stories, or myths, to explain natural phenomena and the history of things that came before man's time on earth. For the ancient Greeks, the creation of the world and everything in it was the work of gods and goddesses. Zeus, the leader of the immortals, and his fellow gods and goddesses commingled with human beings, beginning a series of mythic encounters. For the Greeks, stories of these encounters explained the unexplainable. They illustrated the nature of love and hate, good and evil, war, peace, and the full range of sins, one of the worst of which was arrogance, or pride—called *hubris*. And who better to inspire mortals to display their emotions with all their weaknesses than the gods themselves? To the Greeks, gods and goddesses had all the same problems and personality quirks that humans did, and although they could tolerate pride in themselves, they never could in a mortal. If a human showed too much hubris, it was quite likely a god or goddess would step in and punish that person.

The story of Medusa is a myth that contains one of the earliest mythological monsters, a gorgon. These were fearful creatures, larger than life, who were shaped like women but with hideous faces and snakes instead of hair. Medusa was a beautiful mortal, but after displaying her pride, or hubris, she gets into trouble

with Athena, a goddess often prone to the same weakness. Although Athena is proud, even haughty, no one but Zeus can punish her, and even then, he cannot kill his own daughter. However, Athena has no trouble punishing Medusa for her pride. She turns Medusa into a gorgon, one so ugly that anyone looking at her will turn to stone.

The myth of Medusa takes many different forms as it has been told and retold over the centuries, and she shows up in tales involving heroes and gods, battles and chases. But the single element that never changes is that the once proud woman became a creature with snakes for hair, whose eyes turned onlookers to stone, and who, for all time, represented a frightening, unknown, mysterious entity. If you should seek out and find other stories about Medusa, I hope they are good ones. But be careful—keep your shield polished, lest you find Medusa herself!

—D.N.L.

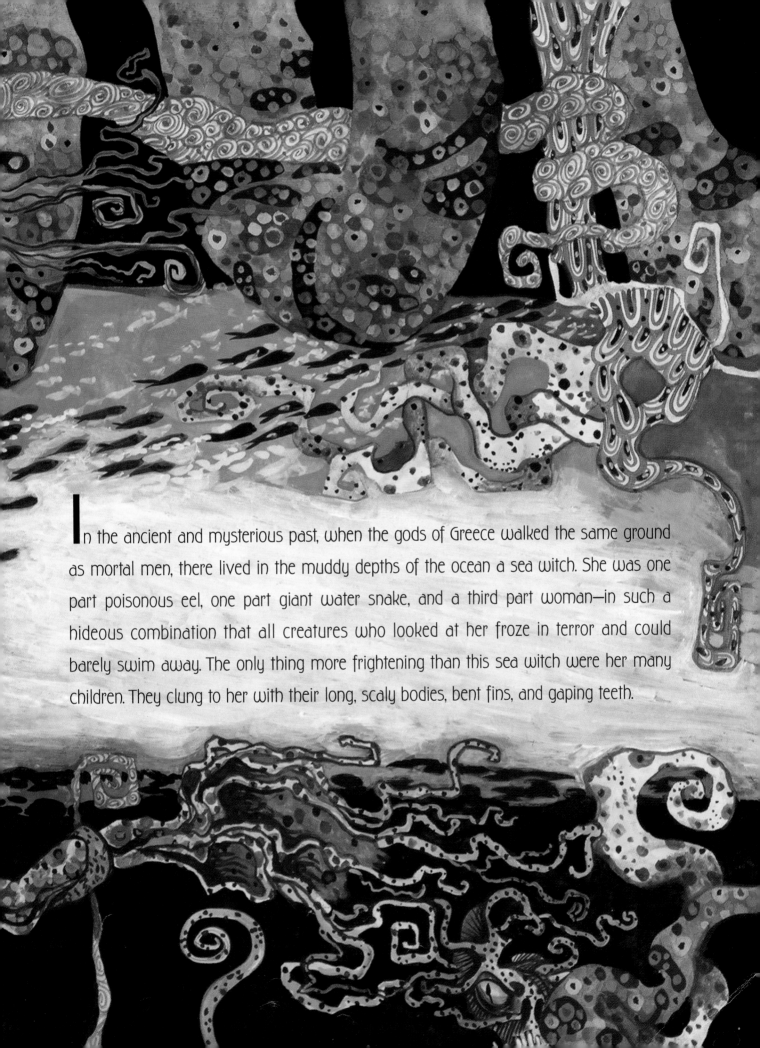

In the ancient and mysterious past, when the gods of Greece walked the same ground as mortal men, there lived in the muddy depths of the ocean a sea witch. She was one part poisonous eel, one part giant water snake, and a third part woman—in such a hideous combination that all creatures who looked at her froze in terror and could barely swim away. The only thing more frightening than this sea witch were her many children. They clung to her with their long, scaly bodies, bent fins, and gaping teeth.

Now, all with the sea witch and her brood remained constant, until a very strange thing happened. The sea witch produced one more child, a girl, and she looked nothing like her sisters or brothers. She was beautiful. The sea witch named her Medusa, and as swift as an undersea storm, news spread of the girl's amazing beauty. Even Poseidon, the King of the Oceans, was entranced. He sent Medusa a betrothal gift, a necklace all of sea gold and pearls of every color.

One sunlit day Medusa sat upon a crag, admiring how the necklace looked against her fair skin.

"I am just like a goddess!" exclaimed Medusa. "I am even more beautiful than Athena herself. And when I marry Poseidon, I will be Queen of all the Oceans."

Medusa did not know that Athena was nearby and heard everything she said. In a jealous fury, the goddess rose in a whirlwind beside the girl.

"You are no goddess," Athena announced, "but the bragging daughter of a mud toad! You came from the sea and to the sea you will return. But only after you live out your days in such ugliness that anyone who looks at you will turn to stone. Hide yourself if you can! One day a boy from the sea will come to kill you. This is my curse!"

Medusa felt a burning, twisting pain in her head. She edged over the crag and stared hard into the mirror of the sea. Her once lustrous hair was a mass of living snakes! She was no longer a beauty, but a horrible monster—a gorgon!

"Athena! I spit on you!" snarled Medusa. And all the snakes on her head hissed and spat. Still too proud to join her ugly sisters and brothers, Medusa fled over land looking for a cave to hide in. And true to Athena's curse, anyone who looked upon her was instantly turned to stone, like one of the statues in the temple of Zeus.

Now, while Medusa hid herself far away on a distant shore, Athena's curse was taking shape. It so happened that an old fisherman saw a wooden chest thrown from a giant wave onto the sandy beach. The salty bindings suddenly burst, and out sprang a woman and a boy, almost more dead than alive.

"Praise Athena, we are free!" said the woman. "I am Danae and this is my son, Perseus. My father was told by a priestess that if I ever had a child, the child would kill him. So my father put me in an underground chamber, hoping no man would ever see me. But Zeus, the King of the Gods himself, saw me through my open sky window. He visited me disguised as a shower of gold and gave me this child. When my father saw my son, he put us in that chest and tossed it far out to sea."

The old fisherman felt sorry for the woman and the child. He took them home and gave them food and drink, and bid them stay.

"You will be safe with me as long as you never venture beyond this cove," said the fisherman. "My evil brother rules the other side of our island, and if he ever sees you, you both may come to harm."

And so, Danae and Perseus lived in great peace and happiness with the old fisherman. But one day, Danae walked, daydreaming, along the inland road. Before she realized where she was, it was too late. She was seized by soldiers and taken away. Perseus saw them and followed close behind, only to be taken prisoner himself.

Athena and Hermes gently took hold of Perseus' arm and flew on an airy path until they came to a small, desolate island. Perseus saw three wrinkled masses—graying creatures with drooping wings and horrid, sagging faces. In the middle of each one's forehead was a sunken hole where an eye should have been.

"Between them they share one eye," said Athena. "Take it from them and do not give it back until they answer you."

"Who speaks?" asked the first Gray Sister. She pushed the eye into the hole in her forehead and let out a terrible screech.

"What is it?" asked the second Gray Sister. "Give me the eye. I want to see."

The minute the first sister removed the eye from her forehead and held it out for the second sister, Perseus rushed up and grabbed it.

"I've got your eye and will not give it back until you tell me the way to the cave of the gorgon Medusa," said Perseus.

The Gray Sisters howled and wailed and gnashed their teeth. Their scraggly arms flailed out, trying to find the thief. But Perseus held on to the eye.

"All right," snarled the third sister. "You must first go beyond the grass-green sea to the Isle of the North. There the nymphs of the winds will give you what you need to find Medusa's cave. Now give us our eye!"

As soon as Perseus dropped the eye into the clutching hands of the Gray Sisters, Athena and Hermes whisked him high above the sea. Soon they stopped on a beautiful windswept island. All of a sudden Perseus heard three sweet-toned voices, softer than a songbird's, and he felt nimble fingers like gentle gusts of wind encircling him. He watched as invisible hands strapped winged golden sandals to his feet, placed a leather pouch on his arm, and pressed a Cap of Darkness into his hands.

"Quickly," whispered the nymphs, "go to the Isle of the Hyperboreans. There you will find the gorgon's cave." Airy fingertips pointed past the horizon, and the voices faded into the evening mists.

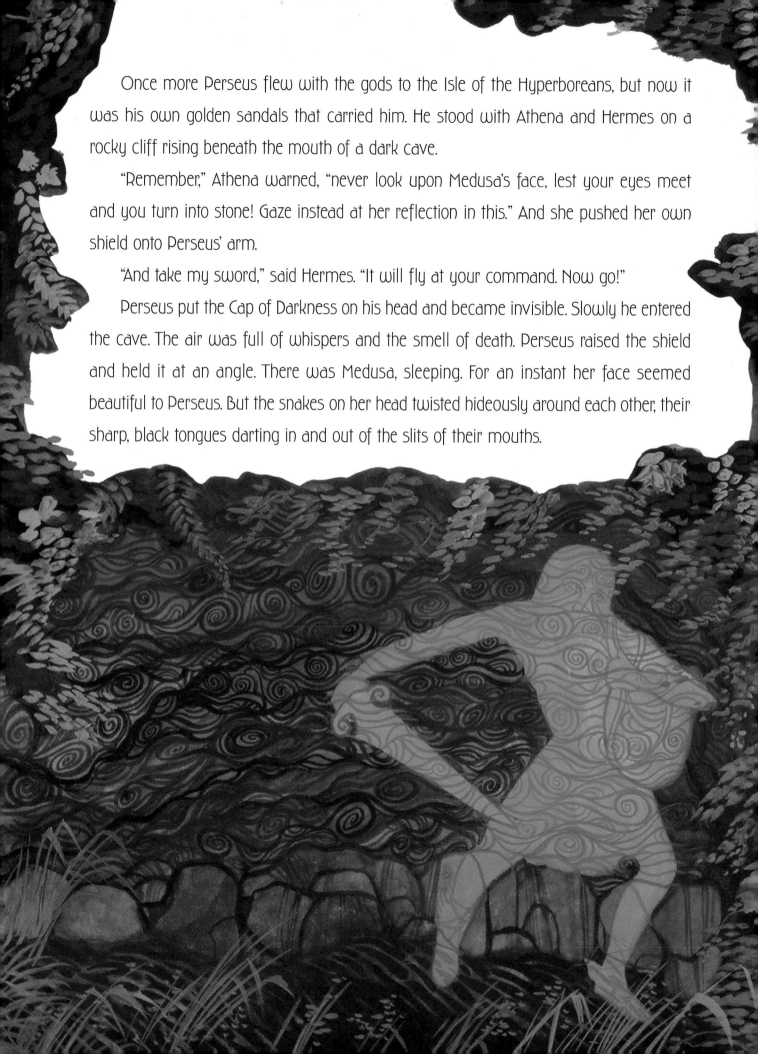

Once more Perseus flew with the gods to the Isle of the Hyperboreans, but now it was his own golden sandals that carried him. He stood with Athena and Hermes on a rocky cliff rising beneath the mouth of a dark cave.

"Remember," Athena warned, "never look upon Medusa's face, lest your eyes meet and you turn into stone! Gaze instead at her reflection in this." And she pushed her own shield onto Perseus' arm.

"And take my sword," said Hermes. "It will fly at your command. Now go!"

Perseus put the Cap of Darkness on his head and became invisible. Slowly he entered the cave. The air was full of whispers and the smell of death. Perseus raised the shield and held it at an angle. There was Medusa, sleeping. For an instant her face seemed beautiful to Perseus. But the snakes on her head twisted hideously around each other, their sharp, black tongues darting in and out of the slits of their mouths.

As Perseus raised his sword, Medusa awoke. Her eyes opened wide. Every snake on her head coiled back, ready to strike. Perseus' hand began to shake as he stared at Medusa's reflection. Never had he seen such a horror, all scales and veins, covered with slime from the floor of the cave. Suddenly, the Cap of Darkness slipped from his head. He was in full view!

Medusa's face darkened with anger. Her eyelids flushed crimson. Her tongue licked at the rancid air as she rose up in front of the shield.

"Athena!" Medusa hissed. "I see your messenger hiding behind your shield. Kill me if you can!" And she lunged forward.

"Sword of Hermes!" shouted Perseus. "For my mother's life and mine, help me now!"

Instantly, the sword came down. Like a silver beam, it sliced the air, and when its tip hit the ground, Medusa's head lay at Perseus' feet.

With Medusa's head safely tucked into the leather pouch, Perseus flew toward the palace of Polydectes. The sun was rising, and Perseus feared he was too late. But as he alighted, he saw Danae kneeling at Polydectes' feet, shielding her face. The tyrant clutched a dagger over her head.

"Stop!" Perseus yelled. "I have the gift you sent me for!"

Polydectes stopped and frowned. "I am not such a fool to believe that you have the gorgon's head. No one has ever seen Medusa and survived. Show me what you hide in that pouch. For all I know it is nothing more than a giant snake!"

"You have asked for it, and have it you will," cried Perseus. "Mother! Cover your eyes!"

Perseus opened the pouch and pulled out the head of Medusa. Polydectes and his soldiers shrank back in horror. But it was too late. Even in death, Medusa's gaze turned them into stone. Perseus quickly thrust the head back into the pouch and tied it up.

Perseus embraced his mother, and together they wept for joy.

Since that day, the old and wise fisherman ruled the island, where Danae lived a long and happy life. Perseus, a hero, traveled the world in search of adventure. And Athena, her anger spent, took the pouch and threw it into the ocean. When Medusa's head fell onto the bottom of the sea, her blood streamed out across the salty depths, and wherever it trickled, the blood turned to bright-red coral, from sea to sea and ocean to ocean. And, from that day to this, the red coral glimmers in the darkest, most frightening parts of the underwater world—all that is left of the blood of Medusa.

To Michael R. Cart, with admiration, joy, and love

Medusa

Copyright © 2000 by Deborah Nourse Lattimore

Printed in the U.S.A. All rights reserved.

http://www.harperchildrens.com

Library of Congress Cataloging-in-Publication Data

Lattimore, Deborah Nourse.

Medusa / Deborah Nourse Lattimore.

p.   cm.

Summary: A retelling of the myth of Medusa, turned by Athena's curse into a gorgon whose gaze turned men to stone, and Perseus' quest to vanquish her in order to save his mother's life.

ISBN 0-06-027904-4. — ISBN 0-06-027905-2 (lib. bdg.)

1. Medusa (Greek mythology)—Juvenile literature.   [1. Medusa (Greek mythology) 2. Greek mythology.]   I. Title.

BL820.M38L38   2000   99-29244

398.2'0938'02—dc21   CIP

Typography by Alicia Mikles

1   2   3   4   5   6   7   8   9   10

❖

First Edition